The Art of Sugarcraft

PASTILLAGE AND SUGAR MOULDING

The Art of Sugarcraft

PASTILLAGE

AND
SUGAR MOULDING

NICHOLAS LODGE

Foreword Angela Priddy
Series Editor Joyce Becker
Photography Graham Tann

MEREHURST PRESS
LONDON

Published 1987 by Merehurst Press
5 Great James Street
London WC1N 3DA

ISBN 0 948075 55 4

Designed by Carole Perks
Editorial Assistant Suzanne Ellis
Typeset by Filmset
Colour separation by Fotographics Ltd, London-Hong Kong
Printed by New Interlitho S.p.A., Milan

ACKNOWLEDGEMENTS
I dedicate this book to my Mum and Dad for always being there and
to Michael and Neil, my brothers, who have given me support over
the years.
My love to very close friends Monica and David, Angela and Don; and
to Jane, Joy and Anne, for all their help over the last year.

The Publishers would like to thank the following for their help and
advice:
Lucy Baker
Briar Wheels & Supplies Ltd, Whitsbury Road, Fordingbridge,
    Hants. SP6 1NQ
C.E.P. Chocolate & Sugar Moulds, 7 Durrington Road,
    Bournemouth BH7 6PU
Elizabeth David Ltd, 46 Bourne Street, London SW1W 8JD and at
    Covent Garden Kitchen Supplies, 3 North Row, The Market,
    Covent Garden, London WC2
Kim Golding
B.R. Mathews & Son, 12 Gipsy Hill, Upper Norwood,
    London SE19 1NN
Guy Paul and Company Limited, Unit B4, A1 Industrial Park,
    Little End Road, Eton Scoton, Cambridgeshire, PE19 3JH
Angela Priddy of Angela's Sugarcraft, PO Box 460, Kadoma,
    Zimbabwe
Moulds supplied by Wilton Enterprises, USA
Woodnutt's Ltd, 97 Church Road, Hove, East Sussex BN3 2BA

The church was taken from an original design by Lesley Herbert of
Romford, Essex.

Companion volumes:
The Art of Sugarcraft — **MARZIPAN**
The Art of Sugarcraft — **CHOCOLATE**
The Art of Sugarcraft — **PIPING**
The Art of Sugarcraft — **SUGAR FLOWERS**
The Art of Sugarcraft — **ROYAL ICING**
The Art of Sugarcraft — **SUGARPASTE**
The Art of Sugarcraft — **LACE AND FILIGREE**

CONTENTS

FOREWORD

In the last few years the artistic display side of sugarcraft has advanced by leaps and bounds, and yet another field is pastillage and sugar moulding, where a scenario of life-like beauty can be created.

Architecture, moulding decorations and the sculpting and modelling of figures of a thousand different styles has brought a wonderful dimension into sugarcraft.

I am delighted to find that so many important aspects and advancements of pastillage are to be found in this excellent, comprehensive book. It is beautifully illustrated, with clear, concise instructions which will have vast appeal to all lovers of sugar art.

Nick Lodge is a leading exponent of his art and is clearly combining fine artistic talent with his experience of working with sugar. He has a wonderful ability to portray his skills so that others may understand, follow and share a common interest.

Nick and I are 'new friends' sharing a common interest and objective in sugarcraft. We strive to pioneer new ideas, simplify known methods and increase interest in this fascinating art.

On behalf of the sugarcraft world, I say 'Congratulations and thank you, Nick, for such an excellent contribution to THE ART OF SUGARCRAFT'.

ANGELA PRIDDY

NICHOLAS LODGE

Nicholas Lodge is one of the brightest lights in the young generation of sugarcraft artists. Although still in his early twenties, he already has an impressive collection of awards for his outstanding skills in the field of cake decoration.

Nicholas studied cake decoration at the National Bakery School, London, where he was awarded the prize for the best decoration student in his final year. He then worked in a bakery to gain practical experience before joining one of Britain's leading commercial cake decorating firms. As principal designer, Nicholas was responsible for producing cakes commissioned from leading stores and hotels. He also taught Australian and South African icing techniques.

He has taught sugarcraft to students at all levels, as well as demonstrating cake decorating and chocolate work in shops and department stores all over the UK. In addition, he has taught cake decorating in Singapore, Malaysia, Indonesia, Japan, and southern Africa.

In 1986, Nicholas wrote *Sugar Flowers* and co-authored *Chocolate* in THE ART OF SUGARCRAFT series. He has plans for more books in the future.

An active member of the British Sugarcraft Guild and the Chef and Cooks Circle, Nicholas now spends more time judging competitions than entering them. He has an ambition to run his own school of cake decorating, so that he can share his skills as a sugarcraft artist.

INTRODUCTION

Pastillage is a popular form of sugarcraft in which three-dimensional figures are moulded, modelled or cut out and assembled from different pastes. Pastillage can be used to make collars or borders for cakes, panels, top ornaments, boxes, cards, flowers, and all kinds of different figures.

There are recipes for several different kinds of pastillage pastes on the following pages. Although it is possible to use any of these pastes for the designs in this book, there are certain practical considerations about choice of paste. Some of the pastes contain gum tragacanth, which is extracted from a plant which grows mainly in the Middle East. Gum tragacanth is very expensive, so pastes which use it as a hardening agent will be too expensive to use for anything but small pieces. It is therefore preferable to use pastillage paste or gelatine paste for large structures such as churches, candy boxes and cake panels.

As with all sugarcraft work, cleanliness is important. Wash your hands before beginning and have a clean work surface and all of your equipment assembled. Pastillage is one area of sugarcraft where speed really is important. The quicker you can work the better, as the pastes begin to dry out very quickly. Gelatine paste in particular has a very short working life, as little as 15 minutes in a warm, dry room.

When rolling out paste, lightly dust the work surface with cornflour (cornstarch). Use only a small amount, as too much will cause the paste to dry out. Roll the paste as thinly as possible. Paste which is too thick will warp while drying, and the finished pieces will not fit together. Dry cut pieces at room temperature. Drying time will vary according to the size of the pieces, the temperature, and the dampness of the room. Obviously, things will take longer to dry on a very humid day. Turn large pieces regularly so that they dry evenly.

Modelled and moulded pieces should be dried in the same way. Dry moulded pieces in the moulds, then release. Small pieces can be placed in apple trays or on foam to protect them while drying and hold the shape.

There are three types of 'glue' for pastillage — royal icing, flower paste softened with egg white, and gum arabic glue. Generally, it is best to assemble dry pieces with royal icing and pieces which are still soft with softened flower paste or gum arabic glue. Always support assembled pieces until the 'glue' has dried.

Pastillage pastes can be coloured with paste colour, or the finished pieces can be painted and dusted with edible colouring when dry.

Store unused paste in a polythene bag sealed in an air-tight container and keep in a cool, dry place. Storage time varies from 1 day to about 3 weeks, depending on the paste and the climate. Finished objects, however, should never be stored in plastic or metal containers. Keep them on foam or wrapped in white tissue paper and place in cardboard boxes. Cake boxes are excellent for this. If correctly stored in a cool, dry place, pastillage figures will last many years, providing a charming souvenir of a special occasion.

Sugar moulding is similar to pastillage work, but much easier for a beginner. All that is needed is castor (granulated) sugar and water, making it very inexpensive, even when creating larger pieces. The pieces can be coloured by adding powdered colour to the water before mixing with the sugar. Moulded sugar can be used to produce sweets, small models, boxes, bells, slippers, and many other unusual and attractive items.

RECIPES

Mexican paste

Some figures in this book are made using techniques practised in Mexico where moulded figures are a traditional form of decoration. Mexican paste is very adaptable. Figures can be moulded from it, or it can be mixed half and half with sugarpaste to make clothes for the figures. The same paste is used for bas relief.

> 225g (8oz/2 cups) sifted icing (confectioner's) sugar
> 15ml (3 teaspoons) gum tragacanth
> 5ml (1 teaspoon) liquid glucose
> 30ml (6 teaspoons) cold water

Sift sugar and gum tragacanth onto a clean work surface. Make a well and add liquid glucose and cold water. Add 5 teaspoons of the water and only add the sixth if too firm. Taking sugar from the outside, start to mix the paste.

Knead until all ingredients are blended. If the paste is to be used for moulding bodies, add 15ml (3 teaspoons) cornflour (cornstarch) to paste and knead in. The paste made without the cornflour (cornstarch) will keep for about three weeks. The paste with cornflour (cornstarch) in it will only keep for 24 hours. If any is left over use it to make spare bodies, arms, etc to have in stock.

Pastillage

This strong paste is ideal for three-dimensional structures such as caskets and churches.

> 10g (⅓oz) leaf gelatine
> 60ml (2fl oz/4 tablespoons) water
> 500g (1lb 2oz/4½ cups) icing (confectioner's) sugar, sifted
> 30g (1oz) cornflour (cornstarch)
> 30g (1oz) royal icing

Soak gelatine in water until softened. Warm over hot water until gelatine is dissolved. Make a well by sifting sugar and cornflour onto the work surface. Pour in water and gelatine solution. Mix. Add royal icing. Store in a polythene bag in a plastic container with a lid.

Flower paste

This paste can be used for many of the items in this book, but it would be uneconomical to use it to mould bells or posy bowls or to make candy boxes. Pastillage or gelatine paste should be used for these larger items

425g (14oz/3½ cups) icing (confectioner's) sugar, sifted
60g (2oz/½ cup) cornflour (cornstarch)
15ml (3 teaspoons) gum tragacanth
or
10ml (2 teaspoons) gum tragacanth
and 10ml (2 teaspoons) carboxy methyl cellulose
25ml (5 teaspoons) cold water
10ml (2 teaspoons) powdered gelatine
15ml (3 teaspoons) white fat (shortening)
10ml (2 teaspoons) liquid glucose
white of one large egg, string removed

Sift together sugar and cornflour in the bowl of a heavy-duty mixer. Sprinkle over the gum tragacanth, *or* the gum tragacanth and carboxy methyl cellulose.

Place mixer bowl over a large pan of boiling water. Cover with a dry cloth, and then with a plate or cake board.

Put the water in a small glass bowl and sprinkle the powdered gelatine over it. Leave to sponge.

Half fill a small saucepan with water and place over low heat. Bring to just below boiling point. Place bowl of sponged gelatine, the container of liquid glucose and the beater from the mixer in the water. Heat until gelatine is clear. Remove bowl of gelatine from the pan and stir in the liquid glucose and the white fat. Stir until the fat is melted.

When the icing sugar feels warm, take the bowl off the pan of boiling water, dry the bottom, and place on the mixer. Remove the beater from the other pan, dry and assemble the mixer. Add the gelatine solution and the egg white to the sugar. Cover the bowl with a cloth, and turn the mixer to the slowest speed. Mix until all the ingredients are combined and the paste is a dull beige colour.

Turn the mixer to maximum and beat until the paste is white and stringy. This will take 5-10 minutes. Remove the paste from the bowl and place in a clean plastic bag. Place bag in an airtight container and refrigerate for at least 24 hours before using. If planning to store the paste for a few weeks, put it in four or five small bags and open one at a time.

To use paste, cut off a small piece, add a smear of white fat and dip into some egg white before working. The warmth of your hands will bring the paste to a workable, elastic consistency. Remember that the paste dries out very quickly, so keep it covered at all times and never cut off more than a very small piece. Certain colours, particularly reds and violets, can change the consistency, so it may be necessary to add more white fat and egg white.

Gelatine paste

Gelatine paste is quick to make and very strong but it sets within 15 minutes of being made. Therefore all necessary equipment (templates, moulds, rolling pin, cornflour (cornstarch), knives, etc) must be assembled before making it, because of its short working life.

675g (1½lb/6 cups) icing (confectioner's) sugar
15ml (3 teaspoons) cold water
5ml (1 teaspoon) powdered gelatine

Sift sugar onto a clean work surface. Put water in a small, heavy saucepan (non-aluminium). Sprinkle with gelatine and dissolve over medium heat. Bring gently just to boiling point, remove from heat.

Use a wooden spoon to take about 15ml (3 teaspoons) sugar from the sieved pile and mix quickly with gelatine in the pan. Continue until mixture is thick.

Scrape mixture from pan to the middle of the pile of icing sugar. Knead quickly as it will start to set right away. Once the mixture resembles sugarpaste and is no longer sticky, place in a polythene bag. You may find it will not take all the sugar, so mix until it has taken up enough sugar to resemble sugarpaste consistency. Sift the remainder back into the pack when you have finished work. Wash your hands and move to a clean area of the work surface. Take a small piece of paste, roll out and cut or mould.

Modelling paste

This paste is used for making ornaments. It is not as strong as pastillage or gum pastes, but can be made quickly.

450g (1lb/4 cups) icing (confectioner's) sugar, sifted
20ml (4 teaspoons) powdered gelatine
10ml (2 teaspoons) liquid glucose
50ml (2fl oz/4 tablespoons) cold water

Sprinkle the gelatine on the water and leave to sponge. Dissolve over warm water until clear. Add glucose to clear gelatine and leave until melted. Make a well in the sugar and add the liquid. Stir with a small spatula or palette knife until well mixed. Knead until pliable.

Place in a polythene bag and leave for at least 3 hours before using. Ideally it should be left overnight.

ROYAL ICING

Royal icing made without glycerine is used to join large structural pieces as it is stronger than egg white.

Fresh egg method
1 large egg white, which has been cracked and left to liquify at room temperature for about 2 hours
300g (10oz/2½ cups) sifted icing (confectioner's) sugar
pinch tartaric acid (cream of tartar)

Put the egg white in a large bowl. Gradually stir in half the sugar until the mixture is the consistency of unwhipped cream. Add the rest of the sugar, a spoonful at a time, stirring after each addition.

Stir, do not beat, until the icing stands in firm peaks when the spoon is withdrawn.

Gum arabic glue
This glue is used for attaching clothes to bodies and for sticking soft pieces of paste to other pieces of soft or firm paste. It will dry more quickly than egg white. This glue does not keep well so make up a small quantity.

Mix 1 part gum arabic with 3 parts cold water. Leave to dissolve.

The same proportions, made with boiling water and left to cool slightly, will result in a glaze. Coat items 2-3 times for best effect.

Albumen powder method
Albumen powder is available in pure or artificial form. Pure 100% dried albumen is used for fine lace work, runouts, etc. It is stronger than artificial albumen, which is only suitable for basic work.

15ml (3 teaspoons) albumen powder
75ml (3fl oz/⅓ cup) cold water
450g (1lb/4 cups) sifted icing (confectioner's) sugar

Dissolve the albumen powder in the cold water and leave to stand for about 30 minutes, stirring every few minutes. Put the sugar in the bowl of an electric mixer, add the dissolved albumen powder, and mix using the beater for about 12-15 minutes.

If using royal icing to coat a cake, it must rest for at least 6 hours to allow the air bubbles to come to the surface and break. Royal icing for piping can be used straight after mixing.

EQUIPMENT

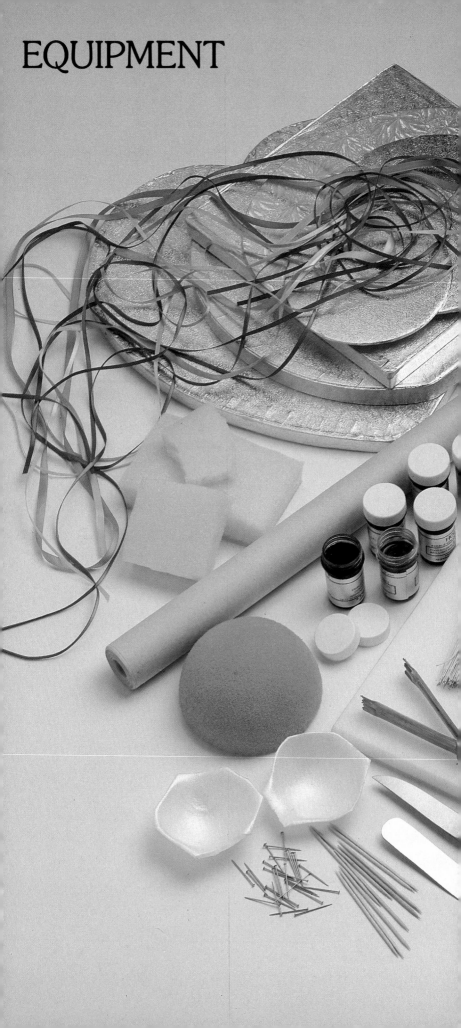

MOULDS

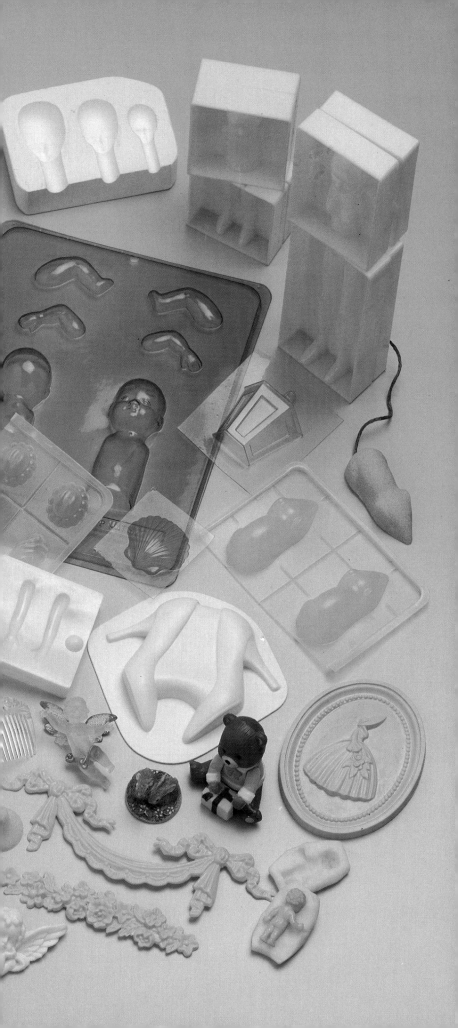

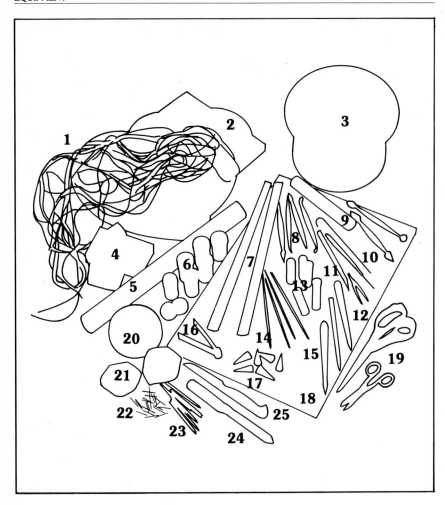

This is a selection of tools and equipment used for pastillage work. Most are ordinary kitchen or household items, while the more unusual tools are available from cake decorating shops and specialist shops.

1 Ribbons
2 Cake boards and cards
3 Turntable
4 Small pieces of foam or sponge
5 Greaseproof paper
6 Paste colours
7 Floristry wire
8 Modelling tools
9 Nonstick rolling pin
10 Scribers
11 Modelling knife
12 Tweezers
13 Petal dust
14 Paintbrushes
15 Anger tools
16 Crimpers
17 Piping tubes
18 Nonstick work surface
19 Scissors
20 Foam ball
21 Apple trays for drying
22 Pins
23 Cocktail sticks
24 Palette knife
25 Kitchen knife

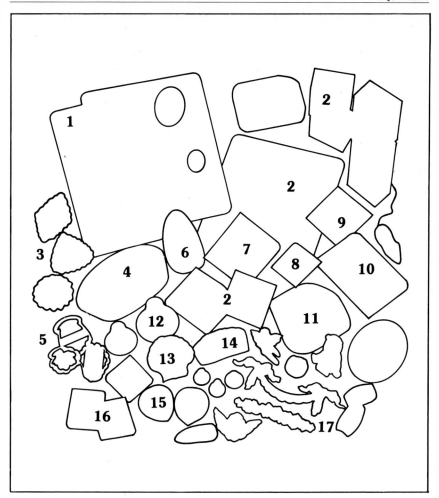

This is a selection of moulds, cutters and equipment for making moulds which can be used for pastillage work. As well as the large selection of commercial moulds available, it is possible to make your own moulds using figurines or embossed plastic objects.

1 Plastic confectionery moulds
2 People moulds
3 Pastry moulds for posy bowls
4 Swan mould
5 Cutters for rolled-out paste
6 Snowman confectionery mould
7 Chocolate mould
8 Shell mould
9 Large confectionery mould
10 Sugar mice mould
11 Slipper mould
12 Bell moulds
13 Sea shells
14 Plastic comb with embossed design
15 Plastic box with lacy design
16 Oven-hardening modelling compound
17 Glass, china and plastic figures which can be used to make moulds

LOVEBIRDS CAKE

This cake, in an unusual pink and grey colour scheme, has a three-dimensional top decoration of cutout lovebirds. The birds could also be placed flat on the cake top for a different look.

PINK AND GREY ENGAGEMENT CAKE

Cover a hexagonal cake with pink sugarpaste. The cake must be at least 20cm (8in) across.

Roll out pale grey pastillage and cut all the pieces given plus some hearts.

To make the double heart, cut out two hearts. Place cutter slightly over one and cut out a section. The second heart will then sit in the gap. Dry all pieces flat.

Pipe a shell around the base with a No3 tube. Stick a piece of 3mm (⅛in) grey ribbon just above shells. Attach frame as shown, let dry 30 minutes. Place birds' bodies in position with royal icing, let dry 30 minutes. Pipe a line on the back and bottom of each dove. Place wings and tails on bodies. Support with foam in the position shown until dry. Add some paste bows and stick the double hearts on alternate sides. A ribbon bow could be added.

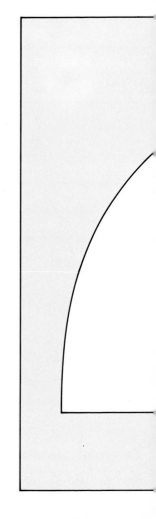

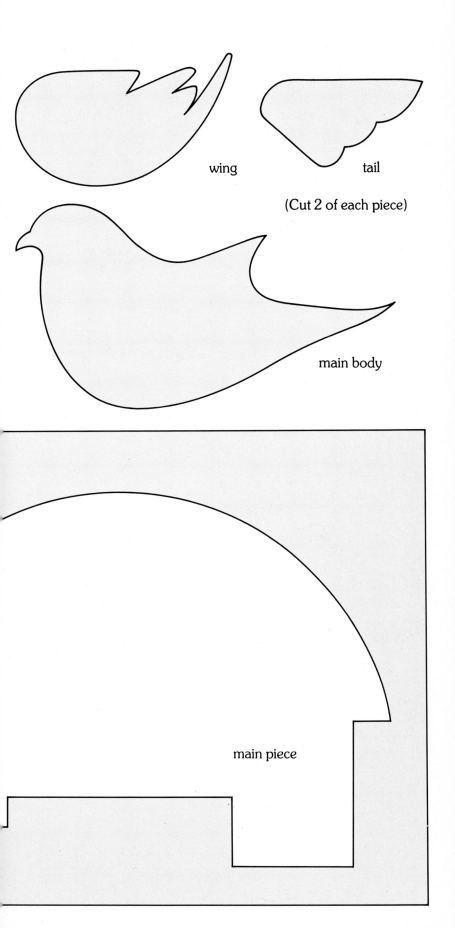

wing

tail

(Cut 2 of each piece)

main body

main piece

CHRISTMAS TREE IN RED POT

This little tree, with or without its pot, could be used on a Christmas cake. Snow piped onto its branches would give a wintry feel.

Roll out some green paste to a thickness of about 1.5mm (1⁄16in). Cut out two trees using a Christmas tree cutter. Cut one tree in half lengthwise with a sharp knife. Let dry.

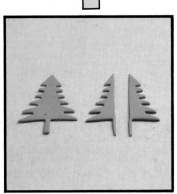

Pipe some green royal icing down the centre of the whole tree. Place one of the half trees onto the icing as shown. Let dry.

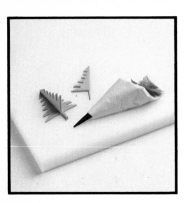

Pipe another line of icing on the opposite side of the whole tree. Place remaining half tree in position. Let dry. Mould tub of red paste and place tree into tub before it dries.

BOW PLAQUE

The lower bow was made with cutters while the top bow was made freehand with long ribbon tails.

BOWS

Bows are a traditional decoration on wedding cakes. These were made using cutters, templates and freehand methods.

Template bows

These are made as for cutter bows except that templates made of thin card are used to cut the shapes.

Ribbons

Roll out some flower, Mexican or pastillage paste until translucent and cut into strips of the desired width. Twist immediately. If draping, as on the clown, attach centre with egg white, twist, drape and attach ends where required.

Cutter bows

Roll out some flower or Mexican paste until it is translucent.

Cut the five pieces required for this bow.

Stick the tails flat onto the plaque or cake. Take each of the two loop pieces in turn, stick in the centre and fold over, sticking again. Finally place the centre piece in position after rolling it into a tube.

Attach with royal icing instead of egg white if you are putting the bow on a royal iced cake surface.

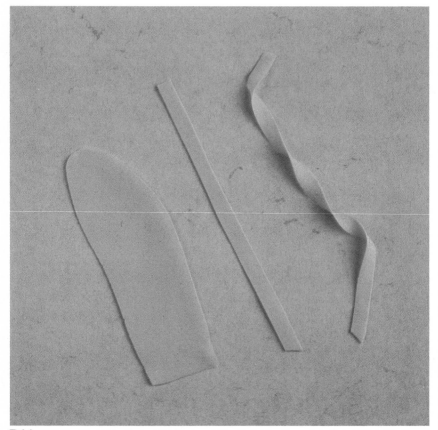

Ribbons

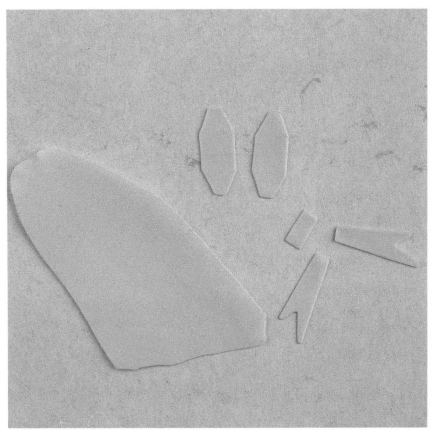

Template bows

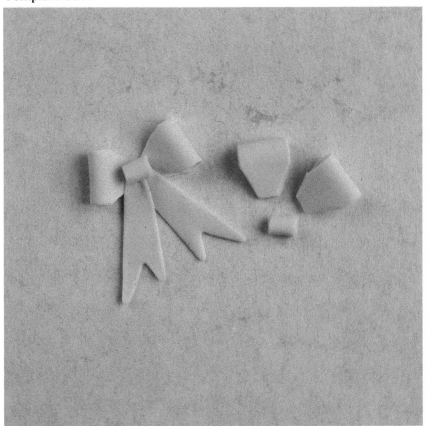

Cutter bows

BUTTERFLY SPECIMEN CASE

A pastillage case filled with pastillage butterflies could top a birthday cake for a man. To save time, a wooden frame could be used, and the butterflies could be mounted on card instead of a sugarpaste plaque.

BUTTERFLIES

Butterflies are an attractive addition to wedding and celebration cakes. As they can be made in various shapes and sizes, they are handy for filling in an empty spot on a decorated cake. Look in nature or butterfly books for ideas of colouring. Once a design has been chosen trace the shape on thin card to make a template.

These butterflies have been made with flower paste but pastillage could also be used.

Make template of thin card. Roll out flower paste very thinly.

Cut out wings. Mark the main centre vein with a cocktail stick.

Dust wings orange with a brown edge. The detail is painted on with a fine paintbrush. Painting on all the detail will take about 30 minutes.

Pipe the body in white onto waxed paper using a No2 tube. Attach wings at once and support with foam. Attach fine stamens as above. Paint body with black food colour diluted with some clear spirit to give a grey shade.

BRIDAL BUTTERFLIES

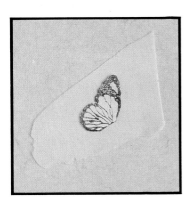

These pretty butterflies can be made in any pastel shade. Make templates of thin card. Roll out flower paste thinly to make translucent wings. Cut out a pair of wings using template.

Vein by placing onto a petal or foliage veiner to give a slight texture. Roll a cocktail stick onto the top of the wing to give movement. Leave to dry for about three hours, turning over half way through to dry underside.

Use a dry No3 or 4 paintbrush to dust wings with pink petal dust. Mix a small amount of green paste colour with a little colourless spirit (such as gin, vodka or kirsch). Paint on the design with a No0 or 00 brush. The alcohol will evaporate very quickly, making the wings easier to handle than if the paste colour is mixed with water. Leave wings to dry for ten minutes.

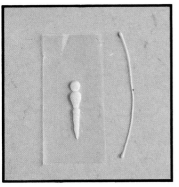

Pipe a body on waxed paper as shown, using a No2 tube filled with royal icing made without glycerine. Immediately place wings into position and support each with a piece of foam. Fold a floristry stamen in half, cut with scissors and place in position on head with tweezers. Let dry for several hours. To finish, dust body with pink petal dust using a dry paintbrush.

Butterfly wings templates

SPECIMEN CASE

This sugarpaste frame with cream pastillage background, made to resemble a specimen display case, comes complete with sugar pins!

It shows the detail that can be put into sugar artistry and would make a charming decoration for the top of a birthday cake as it can be taken off and kept as a souvenir.

The butterflies shown are Brimstone (yellow and gold), Tortoise-shell (multi-coloured), Purple Emperor (mauve), Gatekeeper (orangy-brown) and Chalk Hill Blue (bluish-mauve).

Butterfly wings templates

PASTILLAGE GREETINGS CARDS

Pastillage can be used to make wonderful, original greetings cards for any occasion. The card can be placed on a cake, or it can be boxed and presented as a gift.

A simple pastillage card can be just a flat cutout rectangle or square with a piped or painted message. More interesting designs use cutout shapes, bas relief figures, or, like the card shown here, are in two parts and can stand up. Copy a real card, or draw your own designs.

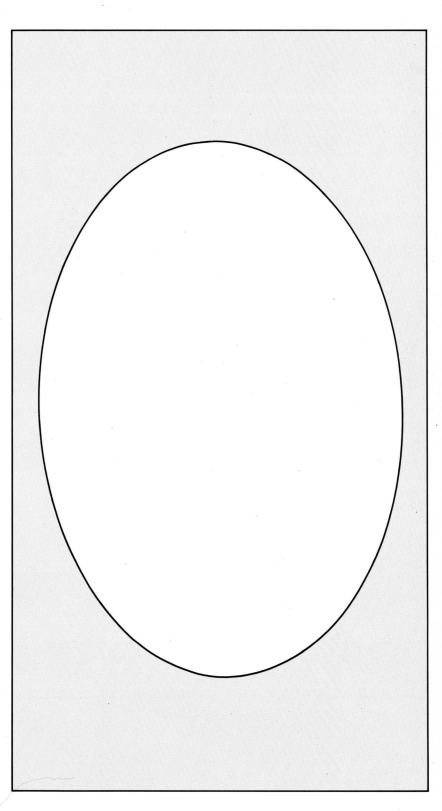

Card — cut 1 solid and
one with cutout window

Roll out flower paste or pastillage paste and use a sharp knife to cut out the pieces following the templates. Leave to dry, turning regularly to ensure they dry evenly. Paint the design on the bottom half. Using royal icing and a No1 tube, pipe cornelli work on the top piece. Pipe a lace edging round the outside edge and the cutout oval.

To assemble the card, pipe a fine line of royal icing along the edge and position the top piece onto the bottom piece at an angle. Support with foam until completely dry. Attach pastillage butterflies, and place another butterfly on the front of the card. Stand up when dry.

FUCHSIA CARD

This modern piece is made of pastillage and flower paste.

Roll out pale green paste to about 3mm (⅛in) thick. Cut out following the template. Roll out some grey paste and cut out using the template. Dry both pieces flat for 24 hours, turning after 12 hours.

Trace fuchsia design onto greaseproof paper, scribe onto the grey plaque. Roll out some flower paste very finely and cut out the petals. Dry flat. Paint on the leaves, stalk and bud using white petal dust mixed with clear spirit and a little mint green colour. When paint is dry, assemble the fuchsia petals on the plaque or cake as shown with a little green royal icing.

Stick the green frame on top with royal icing. Add butterfly, if wished.

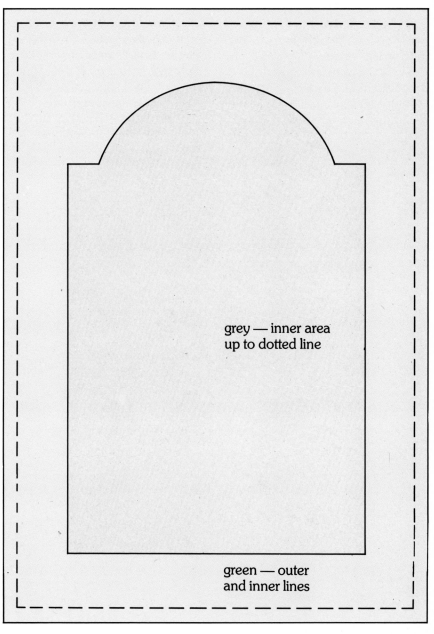

grey — inner area
up to dotted line

green — outer
and inner lines

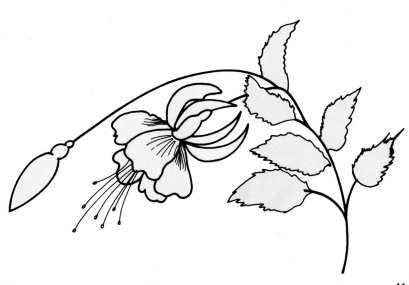

APPLIQUÉ WORK

Spray of flowers
This needlework technique adapts very well to sugar.

Trace the template and scribe the pattern onto a cake or plaque. Paint in stems using a No0 paintbrush. Use green to paint in the small leaves. Trace the pattern for the large leaves and petals onto paper or card and cut out. Roll out flower paste of the desired colours. Cut out petals and leaves. Stick onto surface with egg white, then dry. Start with the flower furthest away from you, for example the pink blossom on the right is slightly under the large rose so attach the blossom first.

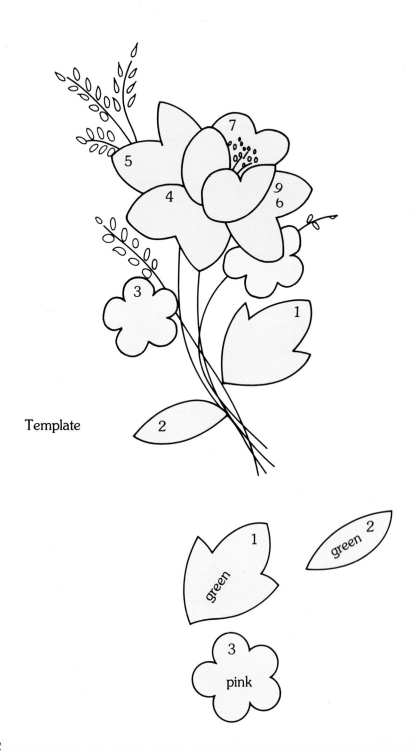

Template

Appliqué work plaque.
This plaque has been decorated
with an appliqué flower design.
Roll out the coloured paste so it is
translucent, cut out using a
modelling knife.

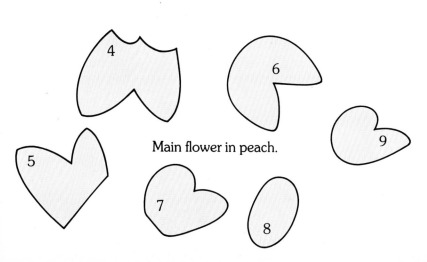

Main flower in peach.

CHURCH

This church was about 20cm
(8in) tall at its highest point. Use
as a freestanding table decoration,
or on a wedding, christening or
confirmation cake.

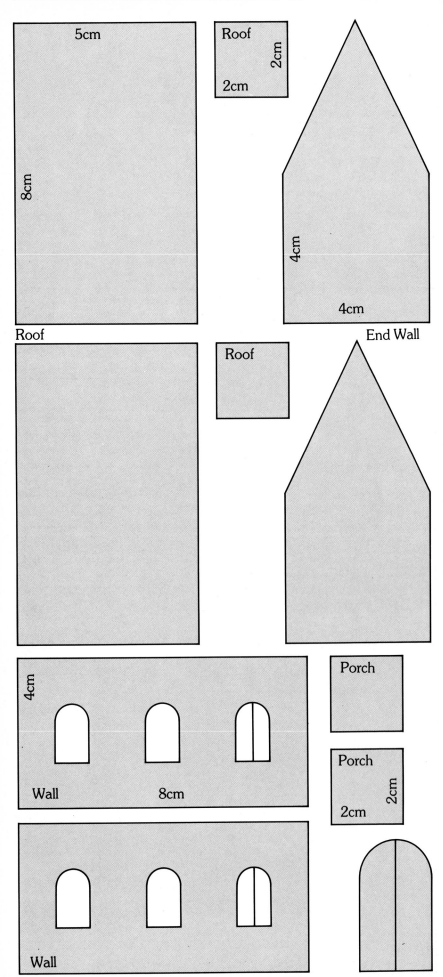

5cm

Roof

2cm

2cm

8cm

Roof

4cm

4cm

End Wall

Roof

Porch

Porch

2cm

2cm

4cm

Wall 8cm

Wall

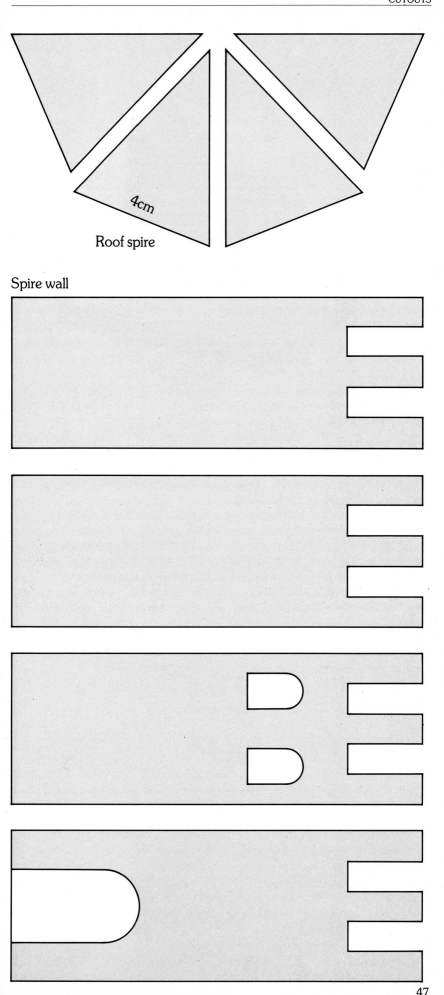

Roof spire

4cm

Spire wall

CHURCH

This church could be made from the basic pieces and not finished as it is here. It also looks attractive in pastel colours with a rambling rose over the doorway. Stained glass windows can be piped in, or use coloured waxed paper, cellophane or rice paper.

Make a pattern from the template given. Use gelatine paste or pastillage coloured mid-brown. Cut all 20 pieces from paste approximately 2mm (1/10in) thick. Let pieces dry 12 hours; turn over and leave another 12 hours. Assemble on a cake board or directly on a cake using brown royal icing. Use plenty of icing on the main seams to ensure strength and support.

Stick one end wall piece down and support it in an upright position. Place first wall to join end piece. Place second end wall piece in position. Stick second wall piece to make a rectangle.

Next make the four spire pieces into a square tower, referring to the illustration.

Add the two spire roof sections to the tower; place them opposite each other so their points touch. Let dry for ten minutes. Place the remaining two pieces in position.

Finally attach porch and roof.

Mix brown and black colouring

PRAYER BOOK

This prayer book can be used for the top of a wedding, christening or confirmation cake.

Make a rectangular template of the required size. Roll out some paste and cut around the rectangle. Place over a piece of corrugated roofing or similar, making sure it sits evenly. Cut approximately 3mm (1/8in) from the template. Roll out some white paste very thinly and cut out two

or three pieces following the new template. Paint a line of egg white down the centre of the cover and stick each page at the centre. Turn over the edges and let dry. Pipe some dove wings and let dry. Pipe an inscription using a No0 tube; pipe a heart and two miniature flying doves in the centre of the other side. Finish off with a spray of sugar flowers.

into some Mexican and sugar-paste to get a slightly mottled effect. Smooth a little icing on one small area of the church at a time using a spatula. Mould various size pieces of paste, squash onto surface for a stone wall effect. Cover all the church except the roof, spire and porch roof. When finished, shade with a little brown petal dust.

Colour some paste grey and roll out a piece large enough for the roof. Mark with the large end of a piping tube to represent tiles.

Make the centre gable by cutting a strip, then cutting pieces out of both sides with the piping

tube as shown. Place into position.

Cut four pieces for the spire and place into position. Mark small porch roof with a knife. Mix a little black colouring with some clear spirit and brush over to give a weathered look.

Make two small crosses of thin strips of paste. Stick on with grey icing and leave to dry.

Spread some green icing on the board or cake with a small palette knife for grass. Make a path, and use a clay gun to make bushes. Trees are cones of green paste cut with curved nail scissors to make branches.

CRADLE

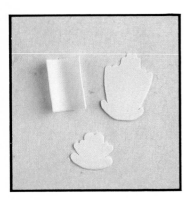

The three cradle pieces should be made at least 24 hours before assembly.

Place the larger of the two flat pieces on a work surface. Using a small piping bag filled with firm royal icing and a No1 tube, stick the curved piece to the flat piece and pipe a small shell on the bottom and inside edge as shown. Let dry for two hours.

Pipe a line on the top edge of the curved piece. Place the small, flat piece into position. Let dry. Turn upright and pipe a shell to match the other end.

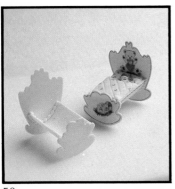

A finished cradle with no decoration stands next to one decorated.

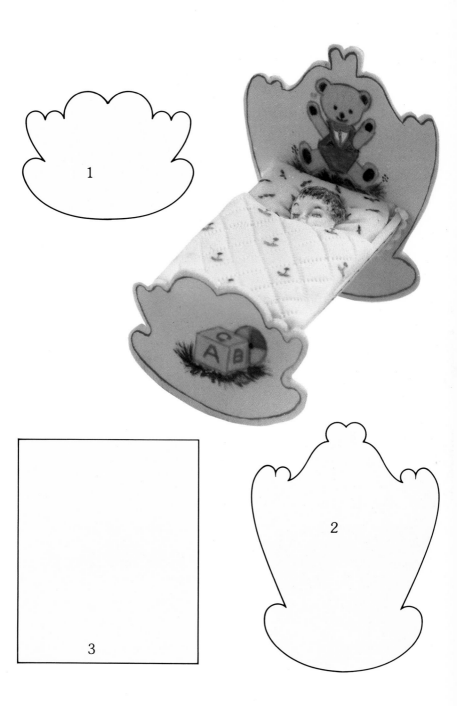

Lemon cradle with teddy bear

Make templates following the patterns. Cut one of each of the three shapes from pale lemon pastillage.

Pieces No1 and 2 are dried flat, No3 is dried over a curved surface such as a small rolling pin or a piece of tubing. Dry thoroughly, turning flat pieces over half way through.

Paint teddy bear and building brick and ball design on cradle and outline pieces in contrasting colour. Let cradle dry. Make a mattress and pillow from Mexican paste. Model baby's face of Mexican paste; dry. Paint features and place on pillow. Roll out a cover, give quilting effect by using a dust comb and then cut to size. Paint design onto cover and pillow if wished.

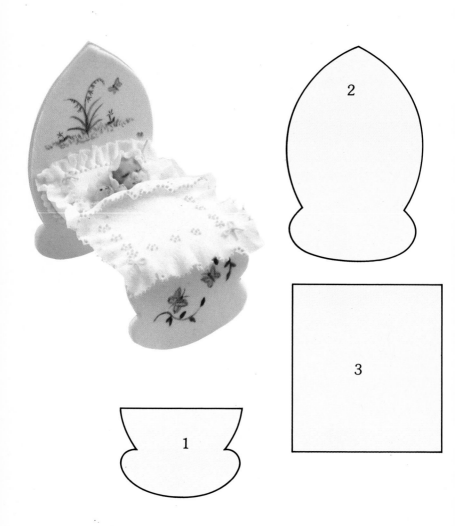

Blue and white cradle

Make this cradle following the directions for the lemon cradle. Frill the edge of pillow and duvet with a cocktail stick. Make arms and head of teddy according to directions, but to miniature size. Make baby's head and place on pillow in cradle. Cover with duvet.

BABIES' BIBS

Small yellow bib with rabbit

This small bib is suitable for a christening or first birthday cake. Cut a bib shape from rolled out paste. Let dry before painting on the rabbit, either freehand or using a tracing scribe to transfer a picture onto the surface. Simple pictures can be found in picture books and on birthday cards.

Paint a line in contrasting colour around the edge and finish off with a bow.

Pink bib

This bib has a freehand design piped on it with a No0 tube and royal icing. To finish, tie a ribbon bow or make one from paste.

FATHER CHRISTMAS SLEIGH AND TOYS

This pastillage sleigh is filled with gifts and toys. Cut out the sleigh pieces using the templates. Let dry, then paint a freehand design such as the holly pattern shown. Allow paint to dry before assembling. Attach the plain rectangular base to a piece of waxed paper using royal icing without glycerine and a No1 tube.

Attach the back piece with royal icing; support with a piece of sponge or two piping tubes. Stick one of the side pieces to the base and back piece, repeat with other side piece. As the inside of the sleigh will be filled with presents and not be visible, use plenty of icing to give support. Finish by fitting the front piece into the two slots in the side pieces and piping a small shell along the front bottom edge. Let dry for about six hours.

Make parcels cut out of coloured paste. Let dry. Make balls, teddy bear, and candy sticks. When dry, use to fill sleigh.

Teddy bear

Colour flower or Mexican paste yellow with a touch of brown. Mould a piece into a ball for head. Roll a piece approximately three times the size of the head into a ball, then form a cone for body. Cut a tiny piece of paste in two; roll each piece into a ball and flatten for ears. Roll another small piece of paste into a ball for nose. Stick head to body with egg white.

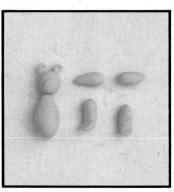

Attach ears and nose to head with egg white. Use a modelling tool to cut two small pieces off the body for the legs to fit into.

Mould legs and arms and attach to body with egg white. Paint eyes, nose, mouth, paws and pads with brown food colouring using a No00 paintbrush.

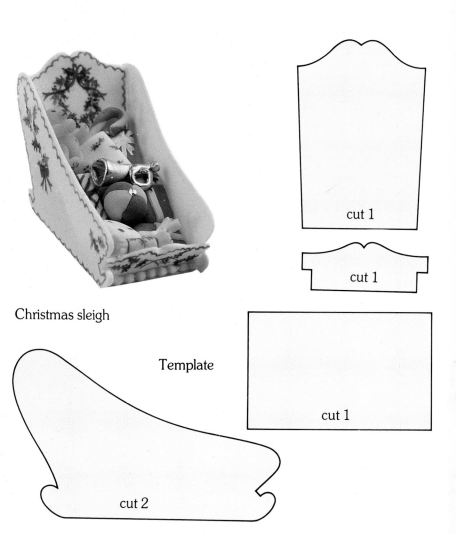

Christmas sleigh

Template

cut 1

cut 1

cut 1

cut 2

Ball
Make this two-tone ball in any colour combination. Take equal-sized pieces of green and blue paste and roll into balls. Cut each ball into quarters using a sharp knife. Make two-tone ball of two quarters of each colour, alternated as shown. Finish with a little piece of white paste.

Candy stick
Take pieces of white and red paste and roll into long, thin sausages. Twist the two colours together. Roll the twisted piece to make an even surface. Cut candy stick to desired length and bend one end round. Let dry before placing in sleigh.

UMBRELLA

Assembling the umbrella pieces over a sponge ball, as shown, makes it three-dimensional. Umbrellas can be positioned on the top or sides of a cake, or as here on a plaque. They make pretty decorations for a birthday cake, and are perfect for North American bridal or baby 'showers'.

Finished plaque

You will need a half sponge ball and some pins. Roll out some coloured pastillage, Mexican or gelatine paste. Cut out umbrella following the template given. Place the umbrella over the ball and support with pins. Let dry for 24 hours.

To make handle and tip roll a long, thin sausage. Cut off a small piece for the tip and curve the longer bit round at one end to form the handle. Dry flat. The finished umbrella has been painted freehand and filled with ribbon loops and flowers.

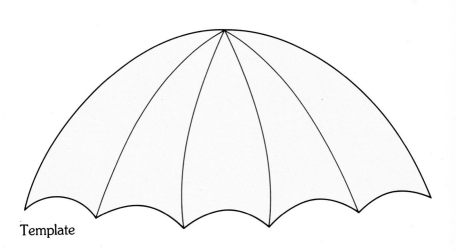

Template

FAN

Roll paste very thinly. Cut out 10-15 pieces using a cutter or make a cardboard template. Dry flat. The ribbon insertion effect was done by cutting short pieces of ribbon and sticking them onto the fan pieces with royal icing. Assemble fan by sticking down the first piece with royal icing, attach the pieces one at a time, each one slightly overlapping the one below. Let dry, paint on a freehand bamboo pattern and add a spray of almond blossom in a delicate shade of pink.

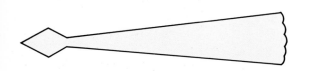

Fan template
cut 10-15 pieces

RING CASE

This oval plaque shows a ring case decorated with sugar lace and a spray of sugar flowers.

Mould two pieces of thin paste over a ring case mould, gently rubbing to produce detail, then return to dry on mould so it keeps its shape. Make a pillow of sugarpaste and place in the bottom half of the case. Place the wedding ring in position and mark some blossom using an ejector blossom cutter. Place case in position on cake or plaque, sticking with a little royal icing. Pipe some icing at the back of the case and place the top in position. Cut a cocktail stick in half and rest the cut end on the cake surface and the pointed end under the lid. Leave to dry. Place a spray of sugar flowers behind the ring case; sweet peas and forget-me-nots have been used here. Place sugar lace pieces around the top and bottom edges of the case.

BOOTIE

Make a mixture of half pink Mexican paste and half sugarpaste. Mould base of booties. Keep paste thin or the top piece will not fit. Stick base onto cake surface with egg white. Roll out another piece of paste to about 2mm (1/10in) thick. Cut out main bootie and stick onto the base, positioning the bottom piece over the pad. Open up the top piece and put a piece of foam underneath to keep it open. Leave about one hour to dry. While the top dries, cover the base with clingfilm to stop it from drying out. Remove clingfilm when top is dry and add four or five pieces of ribbon insertion to the base. Pipe a small snailstrail around the edge and embroider as shown using a No0 tube. Place a small sausage of sugarpaste in the cavity and fill with ribbon loops and flowers. Finish off with a small 3mm (1/8in) ribbon bow.

BALLET SHOES

These pink ballet shoes are made of Mexican paste. Cut out two soles. Stick onto cake surface or a plaque, turning one over to get a left and right foot. Let dry for about 30 minutes. Roll out some more pink paste and cut out the top of the shoe. Stick to base with egg white, starting at the back. When finished, fill out with cotton wool, especially the toe. Remove when dry. Finally add paste ribbon ties. Fill with ribbon or tulle and flowers.

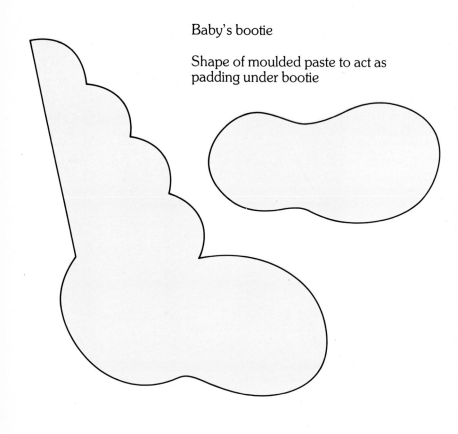

Baby's bootie

Shape of moulded paste to act as
padding under bootie

Ballet shoes

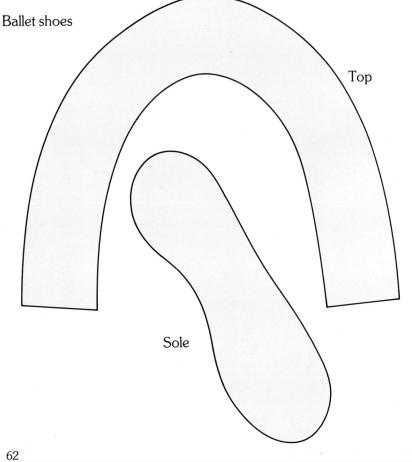

Top

Sole

HEDGEHOGS

To decorate the box shown, make one large and two small hedgehogs. Make a cone of brown Mexican paste and pull up slightly for snout. Cut a slit for the mouth and make indentations for eyes and ears with a ball tool. Mould ears and stick in position with egg white. Mould four feet, cutting each at one end for toes. Stick in position. Mould nose and attach. Roll two small balls of white paste for eyes; place in sockets.

Each spine is rolled between the fingers. Start at the base and stick on all the way round; work outwards slowly. It will take a day to make this top so allow plenty of time. Let dry.

Dust with a mixture of brown and black petal dust. Paint face with food colouring as shown. Mix black food colouring with an equal amount of edible varnish and paint nose and pupils to make them shiny.

BLUEBIRD

Make the log first. Mould the basic shape from brown flower paste, then texture the bark using a needle. Brush with brown paste colour diluted with clear spirit, then shade with dark green petal dust. Dry for 24 hours.

The bird is made from white flower paste. Make a cone for the body and position on the log. The narrow end is the tail; flatten and cut feathers. Cut a few more feathers, curl round the end of a paintbrush, and stick on with egg white.

Make a round ball and stick in place for the head. Indent for eyes. Cut a diamond for the beak. Place some feathers cut from paste on the head. Dry for 6 hours.

Make two paste cones, flatten and position for wings. Support with foam until dry.

Paint the bluebird with paste colour diluted with clear spirit. Dry thoroughly. Position tiny white balls for eyes, dry, then paint with black colouring.

Attach the bluebird on the log to the cake with green royal icing.

FREEHAND RABBIT

Use a mixture of half Mexican paste and half sugarpaste. Model a cone for the body, a ball for the head, two flattened balls for ears, and two sausages for arms. Let dry for a day or two, then stick ears to the head and head to the body. Leave arms unattached at this stage.

Paint rabbit with mid-brown royal icing; leave the top of the body and the arms unpainted as clothes will cover them. Pipe in one small area at a time; brush over with a No4 paintbrush. As icing starts to set, texture with a dry No3 or 4 brush to give the effect of fur. The eyes are pieces of white paste. Mix black colouring and confectioner's varnish to give gloss to pupils. Add a small triangle for nose, dust pink. Stick in some stamens for whiskers.

Dress the body using lemon coloured Mexican paste. Add a white apron, with a bow in the back. Place paste on arms and stick to body with paste softened with a little egg white. Finish off with frills and paint a small design on the apron and dress, if wished.

HEDGEHOG CANDY BOX

A wonderfully impressive gift, this box is made from cut-out pastillage pieces and assembled, then topped with modelled hedgehogs. If stored carefully, wrapped in tissue paper and kept in a cool place, the box should last a long time.

HEDGEHOG BOX

Copy the pattern for the box. Roll out white pastillage or gelatine paste and cut out four hexagonal pieces and six side pieces. (Two extra side pieces are made in case a mistake occurs when painting the design.) Dry all pieces flat. Turn over after 12 hours to dry reverse side.

Assemble with royal icing onto waxed paper. Stick base and inner base together. Attach lid. Paint a freehand or scribed design on the side pieces. Place base on waxed paper. Place side pieces into position, support with sugar lumps or piping tubes until dry. Pipe shells on inside edges for strength and support. Pipe a shell with a No2 tube around the three edges and up the sides of the panels.

On a separate piece of waxed paper, pipe round the edges of lid. When dry, place silk inside box and fill with chocolates, sweets (candy) or petit fours.

Colour box lid with green food colouring. Stick on hedgehogs. Add some moulded toadstools and grass. Transfer to a velvet covered board for presentation.

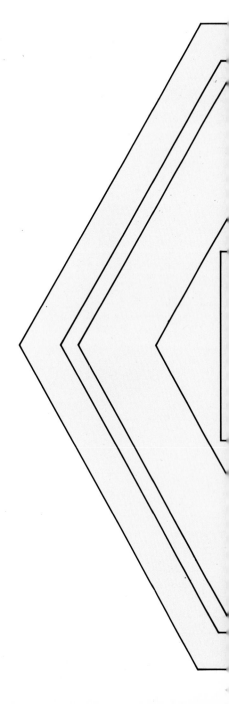

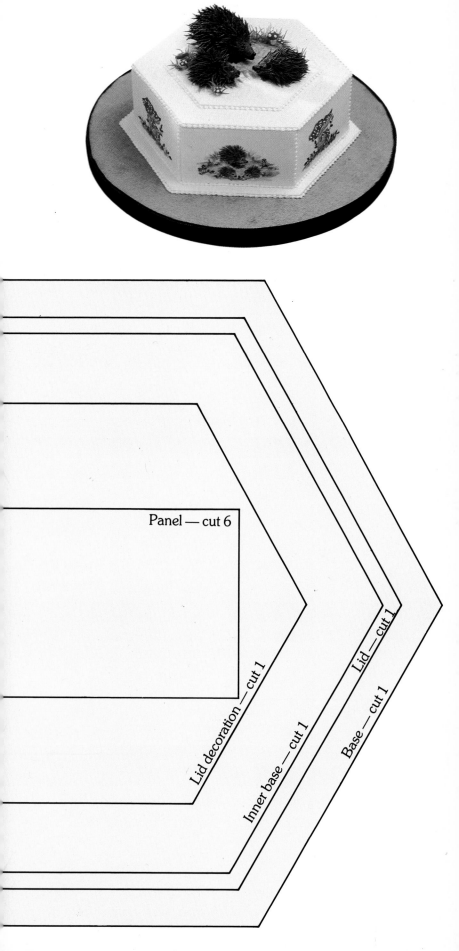

Panel — cut 6

Lid decoration — cut 1

Inner base — cut 1

Lid — cut 1

Base — cut 1

BLUEBIRD BIRTHDAY CAKE

A freehand modelled bluebird of happiness makes a pretty decoration for many different celebration cakes — birthday, wedding, engagement or christening.

GIFT TAGS

Try tying one of these sugar tags to a spray of flowers on a cake. The whole decoration can be removed and kept as a souvenir of the occasion.

Make a template from thin cardboard. Roll out flower or Mexican paste and cut out the tag. Crimp the edge with a No4 crimper or leave plain. Make a hole for ribbon with the narrow end of a No3 piping tube. Paint or pipe a design; an inscription can also be piped. Thread a piece of 3mm (⅛in) ribbon through the hole.

SHIELDS

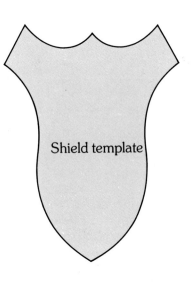

Shield template

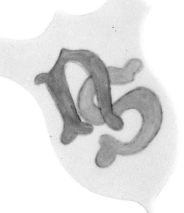

This shield is for a twenty-first birthday cake. After scribing the pattern onto the surface, paint with silver food colour. When dry, outline to give definition. Various edgings could be piped around the outside.

Cut out shield shape. Scribe monogram onto surface and paint with food colouring. Outline in a contrasting colour.

BAS RELIEF

Bas relief is a technique in which two- or three-dimensional pictures are built up of paste on the cake surface or a plaque. Three variations on the basic method are shown here.

Use a mixture of half Mexican and half sugarpaste. Store for 24 hours. This paste is elastic and as it can be rolled very thinly, it frills and pleats beautifully. It will keep about three weeks.

Bas relief can be simple or it can involve an intricate piece taking 15-20 hours to complete.

Claygun. This piece of equipment was designed for pottery work but has now been adopted by sugarcraft artists. Marzipan, flower paste, sugarpaste and Mexican paste can all be used in the clay gun. Soften paste with white fat (shortening) as it compresses under its own weight. Place a small amount of paste into the syringe for best results.

LITTLE GIRL PLAQUE

This little girl was made using the bas relief technique to make her three-dimensional, then assembled on a sugarpaste plaque. The plaque can then be removed and kept as a souvenir when the cake is cut. Figures for this technique can be drawn freehand, or copied from greetings cards, picture books, comic books or children's colouring books.

Finished plaque

The little girl is made in the same way as the clown. The pieces that appear furthest away are put on first; legs before shoes and dress before the apron. Hair is made with a clay gun as explained on page 73.

Template

Plaiting (Braiding). Extrude some paste which has been coloured a suitable shade for hair. Divide into three strands. Pinch together at top and plait (braid). Finish off by pinching together; make a bow of paste and attach to base of plait (braid).

RABBIT PLAQUE

This form of bas relief is very different from the clown and little girl. Trace the pattern and scribe onto the plaque (or cake surface). Brush egg white over the outline and build up the rabbit from a mixture of half sugarpaste and half Mexican paste. Make an eye socket and indentations in the ears. Blend pieces into each other using a greased dresden tool.

Make templates of the basic body parts; head and ears in one piece, lower half of body, and two legs. Roll out some brown paste and cut out head and ear piece. Brush egg white onto the surface; place in position. Stretch the paste to touch the plaque. Indent ear cavity and eye socket. Use a porcupine quill or small darning needle to texture the fur. Add stamens as shown. Brush ear holes pink and place a white eye into the socket. Paint pupil black.

Use the same method for all the other visible brown areas, then dress in jacket, shirt and bow tie made of appropriately coloured paste.

Template

CLOWN PLAQUE

This clown can be made in any colour combination. Assemble directly onto a cake or attach to a plaque. The paste used is a mix-ture of half Mexican paste and half sugarpaste. Sugarpaste alone is used for the basic shape.

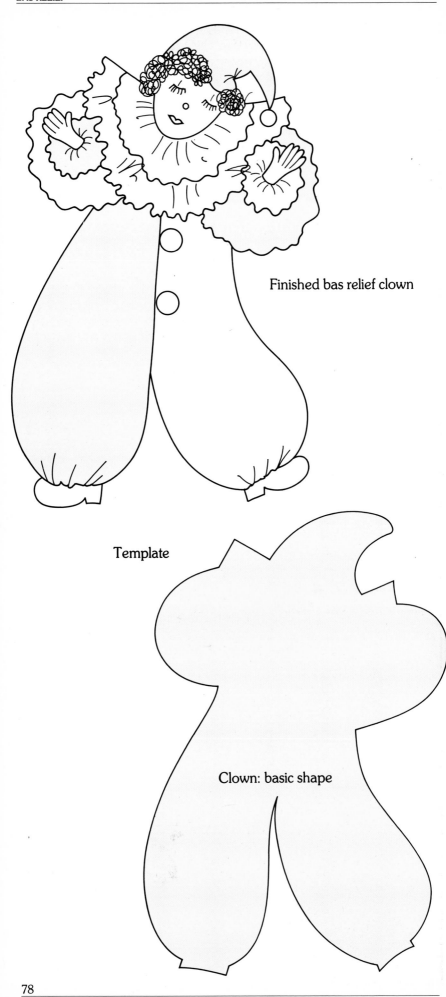

Finished bas relief clown

Template

Clown: basic shape

Roll out some white sugarpaste 3mm (⅛in) thick. Cut out the basic shape using a template made following the pattern. Stick to cake surface or plaque with egg white.

Roll out some blue paste to 1.5mm (1/16in) thick. Cut out the first (blue) trouser leg freehand or following the leg of the pattern. Cut the trouser leg approximately 15mm (½in) wider than the leg at the bottom so there is enough paste to pleat. Cover to stop from drying out.

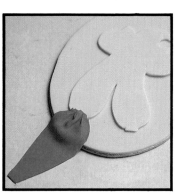

Pleat the wider end of the trouser leg, and using a little egg white, stick as shown.

Brush a little egg white up both sides of trouser leg, pull over and up to give balloon effect. Stick a paintbrush or similar down the top of the trouser leg.

Repeat for second (white) trouser leg. Let dry for about five minutes, then squash the top ends downwards so the arm and neck ruffs can go into position neatly.

Roll out some blue paste and follow template to cut a strip for sleeve. French pleat with your fingers along one edge to make a fan shape. Check against the template to be sure it will be large enough.

Attach to clown with egg white. Trim if necessary. Repeat for white sleeve. Make cavities in the sleeve centres with a modelling tool. Make two holes with a small ball tool for pompoms on trousers.

Roll out some white paste and cut into two narrow strips for ruffles. French pleat and attach as shown.

Roll out some white and some blue paste. Cut out one white and one blue round using a small cutter. Frill with a cocktail stick and place on a piece of sponge. Use a modelling tool to cup them. Make a hole with the end of a paintbrush for wrist.

Make hands as shown. Roll a ball of flesh coloured paste; cut in half. Model each into a pear shape and flatten the wide end. Cut fingers and thumb, place on foam and cup with a ball tool.

Place wrist frills and hands into position. Mould face, using the template to check size and shape. Stick into position with egg white. Use a ball tool to make a hole for the nose and make the mouth with a curved tool.

Roll out some blue paste and cut around hat template. Place hat into position. Pompoms are a cone shape, stuck into holes in trousers and on the hat by the ruff. Use golden yellow paste put through a clay gun or metal sieve to make hair. Place in position with egg white. Mould boots from brown paste.

To paint face, brush pink petal dust on cheeks. Add a piece of pale pink paste for nose. Paint mouth a dark pink and eyes brown using a fine paintbrush. Finally use silver petal dust mixed with clear spirit to paint pompoms and detail on ruffs, etc.

CLOWN CAKE

A charming bas relief clown on top of an oval cake suitable for a child's birthday party. Make the clown in the colours shown, or use the child's favourite colours.

MAKING MOULDS

Years ago moulds were made of sulphur or plaster of Paris. Today new compounds are available which are not so messy or time consuming. The two main choices for mould making material are self hardening or oven drying. The latter is quicker as moulds can be made, baked and used as soon as they have cooled. The self hardening compound is not as useful since large pieces can take up to two weeks to dry. It is also slightly porous and easily damaged.

Moulds made of the oven drying compound are strong and will last forever. The compound can also be used for making decorating tools, such as formers for flowers and leaf veiners.

Knead the compound until it is pliable. Take a piece large enough for making the mould — it must be thick enough to take the depth of the figure and large enough across to take its width. Chose the figure carefully. It should have no cut away areas that would make it difficult to remove after being pressed into the compound.

Form compound into a block. Coat the figure with vegetable oil and press in firmly. Do not move the figure around or definition of the design will be lost. If the identation is not satisfactory, re-mould the compound before baking. Pull out the figure, place compound on a baking tray and put in the oven. Refer to manu-facturer's instructions for baking time and temperature. Remove from oven and cool.

ROSE AND LEAF MOULD

Knead a piece of baking clay until pliable and roll into a ball. Roll out slightly, making sure it is thick enough to contain the item to be moulded. Brush item with vegetable oil.

Push item into the clay, pressing straight down and trying not to wiggle the object as this will make a double impression. Push down until surface is level with the object. Bake in oven as explained on page 84. Cool.

Finished rose. The green paste leaves were put in first by making teardrop shaped pieces of paste and squashing them into the leaf part of the mould. The peach paste was then pushed into the rest of the mould. The flower can also be made of white paste and painted when dry.

BUTTONS

Buttons come in so many unusual designs and shapes that they are excellent for making small

moulds. They can also be used for embossing the surface of a cake.

Knead the clay until soft and pliable. Roll into a ball. Choose a button. Brush with a little vegetable oil and push into the clay until it is level with the surface. Bake the clay to harden the

mould, then cool. Push coloured paste into mould and use a cocktail stick to lever it out. Trim off excess paste with a modelling knife if necessary.

SHELLS

Shells made from plaster moulds.
Sand is coloured castor (granulated) sugar.

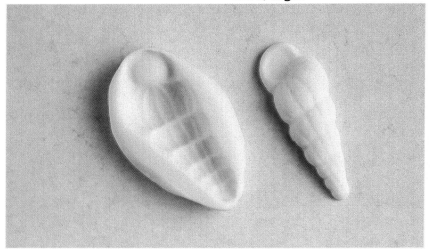

Make moulds from real shells.
Make sure mould is clean and
dry. Dust with cornflour
(cornstarch) using a No4

paintbrush. Press cream paste
into mould. Release paste shell
and let dry. Paint on detail using
brown food colouring.

FATHER CHRISTMAS FACE

Colour pastillage or Mexican paste a flesh colour. Roll into a ball larger than the cavity of the mould. Dust inside of mould with cornflour (cornstarch).

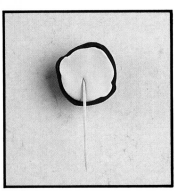

Push ball of paste into prepared mould. Trim off excess paste if necessary.

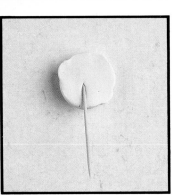

Use a cocktail stick pushed into back of paste to release from mould. The turned out face must be left to dry for at least four hours.

Pink petal dust gives a warm glow to cheeks and nose.

Use white petal dust mixed with a little clear spirit to paint eyes. Finish with blue, then black pupils. Lips are painted red, then outlined with pale brown. Hat is a triangle of red sugarpaste moulded to head.

Finish face by piping beard, moustache, eyebrows, fur and pompom with white royal icing. Use a No1 tube and work on one area at a time. Use a small dry paintbrush to texture icing.
Stick onto a plaque or directly onto the cake with royal icing.

This cheery Father Christmas would make a different centre decoration on a Christmas cake.

CHRISTENING CAKE

The baby on this small christening cake was made using a mould for the head and freehand modelling for the robe. Pink or blue lace could be added to the embroidery on the robe and cake.

BABY IN CHRISTENING DRESS

Mould the baby's head, torso and arms using figure moulds and following the instructions for the little girl in green. Leave to dry.

The clothes are all modelled from a mixture of half Mexican paste and half sugarpaste. Begin dressing the figure by cutting a strip of paste twice the length of the torso and wrapping it round like a tube. This is the base on which to fit the dress. Mark the waist. Cut a rectangle for the skirt and place on a piece of foam. Mark with broderie anglaise and pipe forget-me-nots. Pleat the top

and attach to the baby's waist. Frill the bottom. The bodice is decorated with piped forget-me-nots. Wrap round the torso and attach with egg white. Attach a strip for the sash round the waist. Cover the arms with strips of paste and frill at the wrist.

Place the baby in the cutout portion of the cake then paint in the face and hair with food colouring.

Cut out a round piece of paste and frill for the cap. Add some small frills round the cap and at the shoulders of the dress.

FATHER CHRISTMAS

Brooch used to make mould with finished mould, made according to instructions on page 85.

Press paste into mould and trim off any excess paste.

Finished paste form taken from mould. Let dry before colouring. Chimney and coat are painted red, face and hands are flesh colour, belt and sack are brown. Let dry for about six hours. Then paint gold belt buckle and features. Pipe snow, beard etc with white royal icing using a No1 tube.

CONFECTIONERY MOULDS

These white paste figures show how food colours and petal dust can be used. Painting finished figures is quicker than colouring paste and also saves waste which occurs when too much paste is coloured.

Car. Painted red with black and then silver.

Horse. Painted dark brown with white and grey detail.

Horseshoes. One is painted with pink petal dust mixed with clear spirit. The other is painted with silver dust and clear spirit.

Goldfish. Painted with gold lustre colour and a small amount of orange colour mixed with clear spirit.

Tortoise. Painted brown and black.

Children. Night-clothes are painted with pink and blue colour mixed with clear spirit. Cheeks are dusted with pink petal dust and hair is painted.

Tiny babies. These babies can be used for christening cakes and cradles. Make a mould using a small, plastic sleeping baby. Use mould to make babies of white paste. Paint one pink with blonde hair and the other blue with brown hair.

Christmas tree. This was painted with green colour mixed with clear spirit. Tub is red and baubles and decorations are silver.

Lantern. Painted silver and finished with holly painted in the cavity with a fine paintbrush.

Robin. This bird was painted in brown and red, using a darker brown for texture on wings, etc.

Lady. Background is dusted pink and the lady painted with silver lustre mixed with clear spirit.

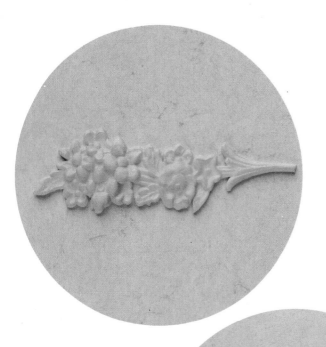

Side designs.
These pieces are
made with special
moulds designed for
this purpose. Several
pieces will be needed
to decorate a cake.

Rabbit. This rabbit
was made using a
mould. Let dry then
colour by painting
with brown colour
mixed with clear
spirit. Shade ears
pink, and mix white
petal dust with clear
spirit and a little pink
colouring to paint
the nose. Stick two
small balls of paste
onto the face with
egg white for eyes.
Paint in pupils. Mix
black food colouring
with an equal
amount of edible
varnish and paint
nose and pupils to
make them shiny.

Painting faces.
These three faces, each with different colouring, illustrate the many possible combinations there are when painting features.

Cameo moulds.
Cameos can be made from chocolate moulds or make your own mould using an embossed object, following the instructions for mould making. Dust the mould with cornflour (constarch) and push a piece of pastillage, flower or Mexican paste into the cavity. Cut off excess. Let dry, then stick the figure on a plaque using royal icing. Place plaque on waxed paper and pipe an edging.

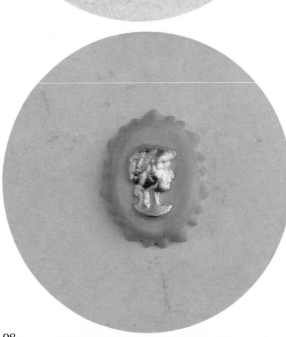

Clown faces.
Clown faces make
an ideal decoration
on a circus cake for
a child's birthday.
These have been
moulded from Mexi-
can paste. Paint on
features with food
colouring. Use
Mexican paste for
frills; roll out, frill
and pleat. Make hair
with clay gun.

Golden angel. This angel was
made using a plaster of Paris angel
figure. Paint with edible gold
colour when dry.

GOLDEN ANNIVERSARY CAKE

This fiftieth wedding anniversary cake features an angel made from a plaster of Paris mould. Paint gold, as shown, or silver for a twenty-fifth anniversary celebration.

On Your
Golden
Wedding

SWANS

For wedding cakes, fill swans with ribbons and flowers; for christenings use swansdown and a paste baby or toys.

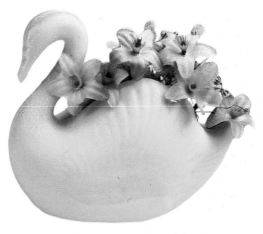

The equipment needed for making a swan. Use Mexican paste.

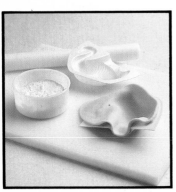

Cut the mould in half and dust with cornflour (cornstarch). Roll out a piece of coloured paste and drape into half of the mould.

Cut off excess paste. Take out swan and dust a little more cornflour (cornstarch) in the mould to ensure the swan does not stick. Make sure the edge of the paste is even and level with the top of the mould. Let dry in mould for about four hours.

Repeat the process on the second half.

Brush some egg white on the soft (second) half and place the two halves together, using paper clips to hold in place. Leave to dry overnight. Take off paper clips and carefully remove moulds.

The finished swan has been dusted with silver snowflake lustre powder to give a silky effect.

BELLS

Bells, plain or filled with flowers, can replace a tall vase of flowers on a wedding cake. Many different bell moulds are commercially available, or make your own from Christmas decorations and even budgie bells.

Use pastillage or gelatine paste. Dust the inside of the mould with cornflour (cornstarch). Roll out paste to about 10mm (⅓in) thick.

Place paste into mould. Push into the centre of the mould. Continue pushing until paste has taken the shape of the inside of the bell. Keep taking paste in and out to be sure it is not sticking. If necessary dust the inside of the mould again with cornflour (cornstarch).

Use a small sharp knife to trim away excess paste. Use your index finger to smooth the edge of the paste to a fine edge.

Leave bell in the mould for about ten minutes before turning out to dry. Leave six hours before decorating.

HALF BELLS

These two bells are half relief, which makes them ideal for decorating the side of a cake. They also give an unusual look to the top of a cake. Careful moulding is important as cracks on the surface will make it difficult to paint the design.

Mould the bell following the instructions, but cut in half while still in the mould, using a modelling knife. Be careful not to damage the mould. Alternatively, remove bell from mould, cut and replace immediately. Leave in mould for about 15 minutes to harden. Remove and dry thoroughly. Paint or pipe a design onto the surface.

The larger bell has a painted holly design. Thread a piece of ribbon under the bell before sticking it down so it appears to be hanging. Pipe in a gong and some dropped lines. If bells are attached on top of a cake, carefully tilt the cake on the turntable so the top of the bell is higher than the bottom, then pipe the dropped lines.

The smaller bell is painted with a dainty floral pattern and finished off with a small bow.

BELLS ON A PLAQUE

These bells have been piped with cornelli work, filled and decorated in the same way as the filled bells on page 108.

This pair of pink and white bells are on a plaque but they could be assembled directly onto the top of a cake. A 18cm (7in) top tier would be required for the large bell.

FORGET-ME-NOT BELLS

Pricking out a design gives a dainty effect on the outside of the bells and is an alternative to cornelli work.

These bells have been moulded. When turned out small forget-me-nots were pricked on the soft paste with a porcupine quill or cocktail stick. The flowers could be outlined using a No00 tube.

FILLED BELL

Use a small piping bag fitted with a No0 tube to pipe cornelli work up to 2cm (¾in) on the inside of the bell. The rest will be filled with ribbon loops and flowers. Place the bell on foam to stop it from moving about. Let dry for about 30 minutes.

Place upturned bell on kitchen towel. Pipe cornelli work over the outside surface; let dry for two hours.

Make some ribbon loops.

Stick a ball of rolled sugarpaste about the size of a walnut into the bottom of the bell. Fill with a circle of ribbon loops, alternating colours. Finish off with ribbon tails.

Use tweezers to add sugar or fabric flowers to fill the gaps.

The bell ready to stick onto the cake top. Prepare some lace, let dry completely. Use a No0 tube to pipe a small line on the top outer edge of the bell; place one piece of lace in position. Work round and under the lower edge of the bell. To attach the lace to the base of the bell, pipe a line, then use a dry No3 or 4 paintbrush as tweezers. Push lace into the bristles, touch onto the line of icing and pull away brush.

The finished bell, filled with ribbon loops and flowers and decorated with a row of sugar lace.

POSY BOWLS

Posy bowls filled with flowers make a change from a spray of flowers on a cake. They suit a two-tier wedding cake where a tall vase would look out of scale, and will add height to a single-tier cake.

Roll out gelatine paste or pastillage to a thickness of about 5mm (¼in). Brush mould with cornflour (cornstarch) so paste does not stick.

Place paste into mould. Use your thumbs to press the paste into the shape. Take out and dust a little more cornflour (cornstarch) into the mould. Replace paste, trim off excess.

SLIPPER

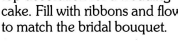

Pastillage slippers are an unusual top decoration for a wedding cake. Fill with ribbons and flowers to match the bridal bouquet.

This sugar slipper has been made with a mould, using the method for the swan on page 102. Once dry pipe cornelli work with a No0 tube in the same shade or a contrasting one. Leave to dry. Stick a small piece of sugarpaste into the slipper with royal icing. Fill with flowers to match those used on the cake. Add a bow to the toe.

Use your index finger to pull from the centre to the outside edge of the mould to give a clean edge. Release from mould. Dust with a bit more cornflour (cornstarch). Replace in mould and leave for about ten minutes. Keep taking it in and out of the mould to make sure it is not sticking.

These posy bowls are white but coloured paste could also be used, or dust the bowls in pastel shades before or after cornelli work. Brush off any excess cornflour (cornstarch) before piping cornelli work with a No0 tube to cover the whole surface. Dry for two hours. If making bowls as a pair, stick together with royal icing. Dry another 4-6 hours.

111

LITTLE GIRL IN GREEN

There are several different types of figure moulds available for making men, women and children in various sizes. The figures can be used on top of cakes, or to make unusual tableaux and scenes from fairy tales or other stories. The little girl shown here was about 20cm (8in) tall; the Victorian lady was a little bit smaller.

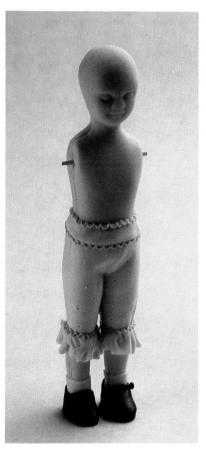

Make head, torso and legs as described. Roll out white flower paste and mould onto feet for socks. Shoes are black paste; cut out a rectangle as shown for top. When dry, stick to socks. Brush egg white onto soles of feet and stand on black paste. Cut round for soles of shoes. Coat shoe tops with confectioner's varnish to look like patent leather.

Cut a long rectangle of white paste. Wrap around middle. Mould the rest around the legs for pantaloons. Finish off by frilling a strip of paste on one edge and pleating on the other, attach as for bas relief clown's trouser legs. Pipe embroidery on surface and edge of legs.

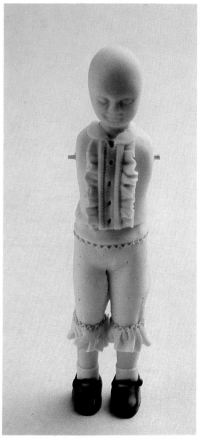

Cut a wide strip of green paste. Wrap around top of body, trim off excess. Frill a thin strip of green paste on both edges. Place down centre of front. Stick a thin green strip on top, make holes and then push in black buttons. A small white collar is attached at neck.

Roll out a strip for the skirt as wide as the required length. Frill on bottom, pleat on top. Place around waist; finish off with a waistband and a big bow at the back.

Make hands as for clown. Stick with egg white into two paste sausages. Roll out green paste to cover them. Add frills around wrist and at top of arms over shoulders.

Make a small teddy bear. Paint girl's face, use a clay gun for hair and make a hat with a frilled brim. Finish as shown.

TORSOS

The torso is made the same way as the legs on page 116. Put pieces of cocktail stick in the neck, the armholes and in the bottom of the waist for support.

When torso and leg sections are dry, attach and leave on foam to set. Use a modelling tool to smooth the join at the waist.

MOULDING HEADS AND LEGS

The equipment needed for moulding heads. This mould is homemade but the method is the same for commercial moulds.

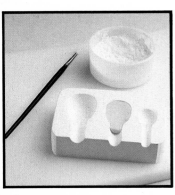

Lightly dust some cornflour (cornstarch) into mould. Push a piece of flesh coloured paste into mould with thumb.

Front half of head, removed from mould. If you require a full head, mould the back. The homemade mould has no back so a piece of paste is placed gently into the same mould so no facial features appear.

The two halves stuck together with egg white. The piece of cocktail stick in the neck will be used later when attaching the body.

The equipment needed to make legs.

Dust mould with cornflour (cornstarch). Push some flesh coloured paste into the front half of the mould. Place pieces of cocktail stick into position as supports, see photograph. Place into a polythene bag to stop from drying out.

Repeat on back half of legs but do not use cocktail sticks.

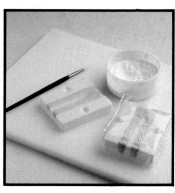

Take front half from polythene bag and use egg white to stick the halves together. Carefully remove both moulds.

The finished legs. Use a modelling knife to trim off any excess paste and support on foam. If changing the position of legs (walking, sitting, etc) do so as quickly as possible so they won't wrinkle.

VICTORIAN LADY

This Victorian lady is made the same way as the little girl. Use a figure on a base rather than one with legs. Dress in burgundy paste.

Make the torso and head from figure moulds as shown. The base of the body is a hand-moulded cone.

The clothes are made from a mixture of half Mexican and half sugarpaste, coloured burgundy. Measure the length from the lady's waist to the base of the cone, then roll out a large strip this size for the skirt. Pleat the top and attach round the waist. Stick a ball of soft base at the back for the bustle, then join the back of the skirt. Frill the hem, and place layers of frills down the front.

Place a strip of paste over the torso for the bodice. Trim at the waist.

Cut two strips, pleat at both ends, and stick at front and back of waist for side bustles. Cover the arms with paste and frill at shoulders and wrists.

Make brown paste hair with a clay gun or garlic press. Place a paste bow at back. Paint in details and features. Add a tiny flower paste fan, if wished.

This type of figure should be used if legs will not be visible when the figure is dressed, ie in a long skirt.

Mould freehand base and stick to dry torso. Dry flat on foam.

An assortment of half and full heads and bodies made with moulds of different sizes.

MOULDED SUGAR WORK

Moulding sugar
This sugar is used for eggs, bells and moulds.

225g (8oz/1 cup) castor (granulated) sugar
10ml (2 teaspoons) cold water

Add water to the sugar in a bowl and mix with a small fork or palette knife. The consistency should be that of damp sand.

If making coloured items, put the colour into the water. It will take some experimenting to be able to judge the shade of the resulting sugar. This sugar will keep in a covered plastic container for several days.

Easter egg
Make egg with a plain egg mould. Pipe on decoration in blue royal icing with a No0 tube.

Sugar mice
Mould in pink sugar using a commercial mould. Attach string tails with royal icing when dry.

Sugar lumps
Use tiny chocolate or sugarpaste moulds to make sugar cubes for a special dinner party or afternoon tea. Try to make them about the size of half a teaspoon (2.5ml).

Snowman and Christmas tree
The snowman was moulded from a 10cm (4in) chocolate mould, using the method described for bells. Turn out two halves. Let dry and stick together with royal icing. A sugarpaste scarf, hat and features are added. The tree is moulded in two halves from green sugar in a chocolate mould and stuck together when dry. Pipe garlands using royal icing and wrap a strip of red paste around the pot.

MOULDED SUGAR BELLS

Mix castor (granulated) sugar with water to the consistency of wet sand. Pack tightly into the mould and scrape off any excess.

Tip out like a sand castle onto waxed or greaseproof paper. Leave the outer surface to dry. Keep checking until the edges are dry enough to hold their shape when centre is scooped out.

Return bell to mould and scrape out the damp centre, first using a teaspoon and then a small palette knife. Continue until you are left with a translucent shell.

Leave the finished bell to dry completely before decorating. The bells can be left plain, piped with royal icing, or filled with ribbons and flowers.

INSTRUCTIONS FOR CAKES

Christening cake. Use a 20cm (8in) round fruit cake. Before marzipanning, cut a narrow section out of the top and side for the baby to rest in. Marzipan, then cover with ivory sugarpaste. Make a rectangle of Mexican paste, frill the edges and place in the cutout section for the blanket. Position the baby in its christening dress, then finish the cake with narrow ribbons, piped embroidery and the baby's name.

Clown cake. Cover a medium size oval cake in pale lemon sugarpaste. Leave to dry for 1-2 days, then assemble clown straight onto the surface. Directions for the clown are given on page 79. Pipe the border on the board using a No57 tube. Roll out blue paste and cut into strips 5mm (¼in) wide. Divide top into eight and use egg white to attach one end of the ribbon. Twist and attach other end, draping into scallops. Finish with a large plunger blossom at top of each scallop.

Bluebird birthday cake. Cover a small oval cake with white sugarpaste and place on an oval board. Pipe a shell border with a No42 tube and attach a ribbon above it. Make the freehand modelled bluebird on a log and attach to the cake with green royal icing. Finish with tiny piped forget-me-nots. Pipe an inscription, if wished.

Golden wedding cake. Cover a heart shaped cake with ivory sugarpaste. The cherub is made of pastillage from a homemade mould. When dry paint with gold lustre colour mixed with a little clear spirit. The top is finished with small plunger blossom and an inscription. The frills for the sides are cut with a plain pastry cutter. Cut each circle in half. Frill and attach as for a Garrett frill. Dots made with a No0 tube are piped around frills. The cake is finished off with 2cm (5/8in) peach ribbon.

Pink and grey engagement cake. Cover a hexagonal cake with pink sugarpaste. The cake must be at least 20cm (8in) across.

Instructions and templates for making this cake are on pages 24 and 25.

INSTRUCTIONS FOR MODELS

Pastillage greetings cards. A simple pastillage card can be just a flat cutout rectangle or square with a piped or painted message. More interesting designs use cutout shapes, bas relief figures, or, like the card shown here, are in two parts and can stand up. Turn to page 38 for instructions on assembly and page 37 for the template pattern.

Hedgehog box. Instructions for making this box are given on page 68 and instructions for making the hedgehogs to decorate the top of the box are on page 63.

Specimen case. This sugarpaste frame with cream pastillage background, made to resemble a specimen display case, comes complete with sugar pins! It shows the detail that can be put into sugar artistry and would make a charming decoration for the top of a birthday cake as it can be taken off and kept as a souvenir.

The butterflies shown are Brimstone (yellow and gold), Tortoise-shell (multi-coloured), Purple Emperor (mauve), Gatekeeper (orangy-brown) and Chalk Hill Blue (bluish-mauve). Instructions for making the butterflies are on pages 32 and 33.

Church. This church could be made from the basic pieces and not finished as it is here. It also looks attractive in pastel colours with a rambling rose over the doorway. Stained glass windows can be piped in, or use coloured waxed paper, cellophane or rice paper. Make a pattern from the template on pages 46 and 47. Instructions for making the church appear on pages 48 and 49.

9